To be Determined

Ashutosh Bagga

Presentation by *BookLeaf Publishing*

Web: www.bookleafpub.com

E-mail: info@bookleafpub.com

ISBN: 9789358731002

First edition 2023

DEDICATION

To Smriti - Thanks for reminding me that I can write even when nothing else is possible!

Wings of Lead

Not every bird is able to fly,
Some are born with glorious wings,
But alas they take on too much lead,
And leaden wings don't bear flight.

For their own weight brings them this fight,
And shaking this off isn't easy at night,
For what's needed is a spark of light,
That shines the night away.

Freeing this young bird from its sway,
Showing him that his wings can still take him
today,
To be where he might find some peace,
For these wings that shone so much,

Were his own creations,
To be born was his destiny and;
Flight - well that's just what it was meant to be.

Masquerade

I don't have the moves,
Nor do I sing out loud,
All I have is my heart for you,
And that I hope you never have to doubt.

Like the brook that broods over its shiny
pebbles,
I do gaze at your blossoming feathers,
Gentle and silent,
But always present,
I watch you grow and moan at the tethers,
For I want you with me - now and forever,
But I am afraid,
To be seen as a masqueraded peasant.

Not that you'd leave,
But I'd want you gone,
For you deserve,
Much more than I can muster.

I Walk

Pathetic yes that's the word,
I feel like shit coz I can't get up.

The weight on my shoulders is debilitating,
I put it there myself so I do know it.

My self is dying,
Faster than I can run from this hell.

And the higher I climb,
Closer I am to the nether.

I watch and I walk,
Each step more menacing.

Every step that I take,
Is closer to my beginning.

To be Determined

At a desk,
Walking down the streets of lore,
A man, a son, a boy, a lover,
What is he - To be determined.

For life will throw and he will toss,
Coz what else can be done,
For a man who,
Is yet to be determined.

Agony and pain,
Are his friends to this day,
For miles he can run but to no avail,
For his finish is yet to be determined.

Looking into windows,
Watching as the world grows,
While he waits for this is his purpose,
For his path - Is yet to be determined.

Sleepless

Staring into this bright oblivion - I wonder if
there are any songs left in me,
Perhaps a note or two still for this world,
Or maybe a symphony,
I stare down blank windows and hope for an
epiphany,
But didn't fortune favor those who wrote their
own destiny.

Awake and yet conscious no more - To my own
self,
As if someone took and stocked on a never to be
reached shelf,
Staying true is harder than just perhaps believing
in thee,
For I have lost faith and it's hard anymore to
sleep.

Endurance

A goal, a determination, some pain and then some more,
For endurance needs nothing else,
A step, a jog and a heart to beat,
Is all that is needed for it to breathe.

No stops on this path - for this is to endure,
Not a man, not a woman, not any breathing being,
An idea that will live on needs all but these three,
A goal, a determination, some pain, and then some more.

Paths of Forgiveness

Into the trees as I go - I think of the deeds I
haven't let go,
Each step that hurts serves as penance,
For miles are still left on this road,
One more and then two - each perhaps another
foot towards the goal.

When will I rid myself of thee?
Of guilt that I cannot unburden me?
I tried shouting out loud and writing it down,
But they said there wasn't anything to forgive.

Then why do I carry this on my back,
As if I am doomed to perish under this sack?
All I want if to be free,
Do let me go - oh please let me be.

Exhausted

Exhaustion, numb, delirium,
All and none,
Breaking through the barriers of mind,
It's all just a state - because I'm not even alive.

Yes, a dead man's words,
What might they be - an old man dead who lived
his life,
"I lived enough - didn't want to no more,
For I felt hunger and also found its cure.
I went around cities,
And made families of strangers,
I lived a life and I need no more"

Now, another dead man's words,
What might they be - a young man gone before
his time,
"It was my time - for I lived enough,
I didn't have it in me to take another punch,
Life came in agony and I didn't have much,
I did what I could for the ones I lived."

Now a woman - neither young nor old,
What might she say - did she want more?

"I was never meant to be, for
something/someone else was wanted,
Yet I did what I did - lived for those that brought
me,
Loved the one that kept me and now when I hear
you,
I question thee - why did you let me be?"

And so it ends the tale of the three - Are they
dead or are they just you or me?

Running against Time

I run, I walk, I pace and then I run again,
Not stopping, not pondering for what I am here
today,
For it is a race and I do not know the end,
And if I stop then I do not know if I'll start
again.

Each moment a lifetime and each year a mere
second,
It goes by as I walk and flashes as I run,
For speed is its friend and sloth its enemy,
And if I stop then I do not know if I'll start
again.

Whatever might the troubles be,
I feel like I can conquer thee,
If and only I sprint and do not walk - as far as I
can possibly on this terrain,
Because if I stop then I do not know if I'll start
again.

Numb

Numb to joy, numb to pain,
Can't be bothered to get up in this rain,
The weight is heavy but it is mine to bear,
Trying to find someone who might care.

This is harder than it ever has been,
To just get up and move through with this
melancholy spleen,
I need some warmth to feel again,
To get up and say that I am alive without refrain.

Moments of Joy

Fleeting, vanishing in a less than an instant,
Desired for a lifetime and then lost before they
could be cherished,
Moments of joy that give life its meaning,
Are rare and far in between but nonetheless
precious more than anything.

Whoever asked to live you in the moment,
Doesn't perhaps understand the value of those
memories,
Each giving life its meaning and the drive to
hope,
For what else is there that if not a moment to
carry against all that needs you to cope.

Yellow Flowers of Fulfillment

A small keepsake to cherish a memory,
Can be worth so much against everything that is
so dreary,
Something won after some hard work,
For no one else but your dumb luck.

A momento if you must,
Found under a tree, unblemished from dust,
Pretty as any stone found in the depth of a mine,
For this means more than even the finest wine.

Won after a battle with your own mind,
Who ever thought a yellow flower could ever be
so kind,
It's not yours to own for its would only last a
moment,
For this is what is nature's covenant.

Days of Old

Memories of a time gone by,
Lived in simpler moments with no need for
pretensions,
Walks with someone that you could count,
It didn't matter because we didn't have any hills
to mount.

Just a moment or two,
And not a lifetime to think about,
Where we didn't have silvers to worry,
For we lived our lives only to be merry.

I look back on those days,
Where we ran not from our problems,
But from a friend,
Looking not for a second to pretend.

The Sea

Gentle and calm, throwing about a feather,
'My friend,' it calls me and takes me into the
Nether,
For under its a wave, a calm ensues,
Where noise there is none but only a pale blue
hue.

It wrestles with me and tosses me away,
But as a boy to his mother I am held in its fray,
For I could spend an eternity in its palm,
I have been held in hypnosis by its charm.

Bones

Push. Push. Push - for you need to reach the
summit,
It's almost here my friend just past your limit,
Your muscles may ache and your bones cry out,
But do not be afraid - for it's not just for some
clout.

Run. Run. Run - for your finish line is here,
Just past your sorrows that you left back in the
rear,
Do not stop and do not let go,
When it's all said and done - you'll be your own
hero.

Efforts in Vain

Some moves are not for glory or fame,
Steps in no direction,
With no one to blame,
Each mile a bit longer in trepidation.

Of the fear that there is podium to climb,
Not a second goes by when you are not on the
grind,
Fear that reminds you that you are no in your
prime,
Each day that goes by you being left behind.

Wake up my friend for you have more to offer,
Life isn't a race nor is it only worth in copper,
Go for what relieves your heart of some pain,
And walk slowly on days and take in the rain.

Truth

In truth we believe but do not often
acknowledge,
The lives we live aren't what we promised.
If we were put on a stand,
And asked for proof,
Would we have enough to show that we weren't
left a fool?

That we do everyday what we say we aspire,
Is a truth that isn't easy to transpire,
We live our lives in the comfort of now,
Accepting what we get from life's poignant
morrow.
Would we stand up now and take up arms for
ourselves?

A self that is lost in the day's pretense,
I implore you dear friend to find a small corner,
Where you did not come as a lonely mourner,
Find what is yours and keep it safe,
Would you like to lose the one thing that kept
you sane?

Things we ought to Say

Words and deeds are all fine and good,
Until we lose sight of the ones we ought not to,
For in saying things we forget sometime,
That we didn't hear a heart's melancholy chime.

It's not for a lack of care or love,
But just being heard is not enough,
For we ought to say to ones we hold dear,
To speak their mind for us to hear.

In things not heard or said,
Are lost life's most splendid threads,
Reeling from a losses we drift away,
Waiting for some words we couldn't say.